GERTRUDE AND ALICE

GERTRUDE AND ALICE

Conceived and created by the Independent Aunties
(*Karin Randoja, Evalyn Parry and Anna Chatterton*)

Written by Anna Chatterton and Evalyn Parry,
in collaboration with Karin Randoja,
with additional text by Gertrude Stein and Alice B. Toklas

PLAYWRIGHTS CANADA PRESS
Toronto

LIBRARY AND ARCHIVES CANADA CATALOGUING IN PUBLICATION
Chatterton, Anna, 1975-, author
    Gertrude and Alice / written by Anna Chatterton and Evalyn Parry, in collaboration with Karin Randoja. -- First edition.

A play.
Issued in print and electronic formats.
ISBN 978-1-77091-880-1 (softcover).--ISBN 978-1-77091-881-8 (PDF).--ISBN 978-1-77091-882-5 (EPUB).--ISBN 978-1-77091-883-2 (Kindle)

    I. Parry, Evalyn, author II. Randoja, Karin, collaborator III. Title.

PS8605.H3925G47 2018   C812'.6   C2017-907541-1
                                               C2017-907542-X

Playwrights Canada Press acknowledges that we operate on land which, for thousands of years, has been the traditional territories of the Mississaugas of the New Credit, the Huron-Wendat, the Anishinaabe, Métis, and the Haudenosaunee peoples. Today, this meeting place is still home to many Indigenous people from across Turtle Island and we are grateful to have the opportunity to work and play here.

We acknowledge the financial support of the Canada Council for the Arts—which last year invested $153 million to bring the arts to Canadians throughout the country—the Ontario Arts Council (OAC), the Ontario Media Development Corporation and the Government of Canada for our publishing activities.

 Canada Council Conseil des arts
for the Arts   du Canada

 ONTARIO ARTS COUNCIL
CONSEIL DES ARTS DE L'ONTARIO
an Ontario government agency
un organisme du gouvernement de l'Ontario

 Canadä

 Ontario
Ontario Media Development
Corporation

For Gertrude Stein and Alice B. Toklas
and all the transgressive female artists
still stubbornly taking space.

INTRODUCTION

The creator of the new composition in the arts is an outlaw until he is a classic.
—Gertrude Stein (1874–1946)

It will take her years to understand the things she's said tonight.
—Alice B. Toklas (1877–1967)

This play is the result of a layered collaboration between us and our historical, larger-than-life subjects Gertrude Stein and Alice B. Toklas. Through our long, deep dive into research and creation, we fell under the spell of these two wonderful, eccentric and transgressive women. Gertrude and Alice came to provide a powerful inspiration for us: challenging us to articulate the meaning(s) of their lives in the context of our own lived experience as contemporary female artists.

An influential literary couple, Gertrude and Alice initially became known for their weekly artist salons at their home in Paris in the 1920s. They were friends of notable modernist painters like Pablo Picasso and Henri Matisse, collecting their art and supporting them early in their careers. Gertrude Stein was a prolific writer. Now credited as one of the major figures of the modernist movement, she was a woman of enormous and unflagging ambition on a quest for literary reinvention. She sought to break down the English language and its conventions and to invent a more accurate and visceral expression for the twentieth century, unobstructed by punctuation or grammatical syntax. In her own lifetime, much of Stein's literary work was the object of ridicule; in fact, until her bestselling book *The Autobiography of Alice B. Toklas* (published in 1933 when Stein was fifty-nine years old), she received very little positive critical attention for her writing. But she was never deterred by what people thought. Staunchly assured of her own literary genius and determined that she should be recognized as such, Gertrude toiled for years in obscurity—although, it must be noted, never in poverty, as family trust funds afforded her and Alice a comfortable lifestyle.

Alice B. Toklas was Gertrude's helpmeet and pragmatic alter ego: lover, typist, editor, cook, household manager and artistic champion, never wavering in her support for Gertrude's often impenetrable, experimental literary works. She called Gertrude her husband and at gatherings was relegated to chatting with the wives. At first glance their relationship seems to suggest a disturbing servitude, yet on closer examination appears to have held mutually satisfying, symbiotic roles for both parties. Alice devoted herself to the creation of a domestic life that allowed Gertrude's creative genius to flourish, managing all their daily domestic affairs, controlling their social calendar and helping see to the publication of Gertrude's work. After Gertrude's death at age seventy-two, Alice spent her remaining years ensuring that all of Gertrude's work be published. At the urging of her community, she also (reluctantly) published two of her own books after Gertrude's death: *The Alice B. Toklas Cookbook* and *What is Remembered*: volumes that reveal Alice's own highly entertaining and erudite literary voice.

Examining their lives, we have been struck over and over again by the complexity of the place and time they lived as women, lesbians, Jews, artists, ex-patriots, exiles and, ultimately, celebrities. In her lifetime Gertrude was an artist who insisted on consorting only with male "geniuses"; she was socially conservative in certain surprising ways: she did not sympathize with the women's suffrage movement, nor did Gertrude and Alice align themselves with the lesbian salons and subculture that existed in Paris at that time. A high-profile Jewish lesbian couple—with little or no allegiance to either of these identities—they somehow survived not only the First but also the Second World War in occupied France.

We wonder what Stein and Toklas would think of the fact that today it is contemporary feminist, queer, Jewish and academic communities who have helped bring Stein the posthumous recognition of literary "genius" she and Alice always believed her to be. Would they be pleased? Would they feel pigeonholed or marginalized in the way history has positioned them? What would they think of us, three female artists who dared not only to portray them but also to inhabit their voices and reinterpret their words? What is remembered and who remembers? The names Gertrude Stein and Alice B. Toklas remain known, but few today have read them (unlike contemporary peers Ernest Hemingway and Picasso, whose names *and* work have endured in the mainstream lexicon). Before we began our research, we ourselves knew very little about Stein's work, life and true significance as an artist and thinker. The deeper our research took us, the more impassioned we became to assert the significance and impact of these two women's work and their important place in Western cultural history.

Our play strives to balance experiments in text and style with narrative and emotional truth. Inspired by Gertrude—who primarily wrote experimental material but eventually (with *The Autobiography*) also produced highly accessible, funny and populist works—we strove to embody some of the riddles and challenges her work presents in the form and content of our production.

As poet and Stein scholar Joan Retallack asks, "How does one develop a contemporary aesthetic, a way of being an artist who connects with the unprecedented character of one's times? [Stein's] starting principle was that we must meet the contemporary moment on its terms—not in ignorance of history but in informed composition of it. Is there any aspect of one's work that poses greater difficulty?"*

Before the play ends—and Gertrude and Alice depart from whence they came—we ask: Can a life lived fully, with attentiveness to the present moment, be enough? Can the experience of being witnessed and heard by a contemporary audience grant Gertrude and Alice some closure and resolution about their legacy, the meaning of their lives and work?

As contemporary creators—as writers, artists, women, secular Jews, lesbians, queers, outsiders ourselves—we believe Gertrude and Alice have something real and relevant to share with us now. Just as Gertrude Stein strove to record and express the "continuous present" in her writing, so we strive to do the same thing, in our own time, with this play: to use these historical characters to unpack and articulate this very moment in which we are alive.

We hope they will inspire you, as they have inspired us.

—Evalyn Parry, Anna Chatterton, Karin Randoja

* Joan Retallack, *The Poethical Wager* (Oakland: University of California Press, 2003), 18.

Gertrude and Alice premiered on March 5, 2016, at Buddies in Bad Times Theatre, Toronto, as a co-production between the Independent Aunties and Buddies in Bad Times with the following cast and creative team:

Gertrude: Evalyn Parry
Alice: Anna Chatterton

Directed and dramaturged by Karin Randoja
Set and video design by Trevor Schwellnus
Lighting design by Michelle Ramsay
Costume design by Ming Wong
Sound design by Christopher Stanton
Props by Jenny So
Stage management by Christina Cicko
"Cahier" program design by Kilby Smith-McGregor
Production management by Charissa Wilcox

The production was nominated for Dora Mavor Moore Awards for Outstanding New Play, Outstanding Ensemble and won for Outstanding Costume Design.

A NOTE ON CREATION, SOURCE MATERIAL AND QUOTATIONS

Gertrude and Alice was conceived and created by the Independent Aunties: Karin Randoja, Evalyn Parry and Anna Chatterton. The play text was written by Anna Chatterton and Evalyn Parry, in collaboration with Karin Randoja, with additional text by Gertrude Stein and Alice B. Toklas. Stein and Toklas's work is now in the public domain in Canada, and we are grateful for the opportunity to use their words, in conversation with our own, to tell this story. All quotations from Stein and Toklas appear in *italics* in the script. Our research and source material includes both of Toklas's books and many of Stein's, as well as numerous biographical works, most significantly *Gertrude and Alice* by Diana Souhami and *Two Lives* by Janet Malcolm. We are grateful to Stein, Toklas, their fans and biographers for the tremendous body of work we have had the opportunity to draw upon in creating our play.

CHARACTERS

Gertrude Stein: has a mid-Atlantic accent, a large girth and takes up plenty of space while radiating intensity and incredible charm.

Alice B. Toklas: chain-smokes, has a lisp and a visible mustache, a reserved physicality and severe yet energetic manner.

SETTING

A theatre. The continuous present.

The characters are aware of the audience at all times.

GERTRUDE and ALICE make a grand entrance—GERTRUDE first
as ALICE shadows behind. GERTRUDE observes the audience.

GERTRUDE

To begin with *thank you very much for everything and of course every-*
one is very welcome.
I declare I do declare it has always been a pleasure.
It is a pleasure seeing you seeing me seeing you.

Who are you? Why are you? When are you?
And where are you?
It has always been a puzzle.
Because right in front of us is the whole story.

I am a woman and my name is Gertrude, Gertrude is my name.
Why am I a woman and why is my name Gertrude?
And when am I a woman and when is my name Gertrude?
And where am I a woman and where is my name Gertrude?
And which woman am I, the woman named Gertrude, which
woman named Gertrude?

Begin again and concentrate.

I am a woman and my name is Gertrude, Gertrude is my name.
And why am I a woman and why is my name Gertrude?

And when am I a woman and when is my name Gertrude?

She laughs.

All right, anyway. You know who this is.

Think of the Bible and Homer, think of Shakespeare and think of me.

This is Gertrude Stein, the most important literary mind of the twentieth century.

And this *(gesturing to* ALICE*)* is Alice B. Toklas. *She is my secretary and the one who makes life comfortable for me.*

But to return to the occasion of being here tonight with you. And what a pleasure it is.

I am curious, it is such a pleasure to have you here and I am curious to know, I am indeed quite curious to know . . . how many of you here have read all of my books— All of my printed and published words . . . I am sure a great number of you have read me . . . but it would be such a pleasure to see how many of you, just how many of you have read ALL of me . . . a show of hands?

She looks around—not many, if any, hands. She reacts without surprise.

A hand? Is there one? No, yes, no, no *(searching the crowd)* I see . . . well anyway, anyway well. I did indeed write a great many great books and so I will lower the bar—the bar that is all of me and—

All right well, well anyway. I want to know who here has read . . . three of my books.

Anyone anyone?

She looks for a show of hands . . .

Yes well anyway well, well anyway, anyway well, anyway, this is the eventuality that we had come to expect and although it is not of course the way we would like things to be of course we have come prepared.

As you may have discovered there are extensive notes authored by myself and the inimitable Alice B. Toklas, which will give you the autobiographical and historical context that you may be lacking since you are clearly more or less and by more or less I obviously mean less familiar with my work than would have been desired.

And yet and yet you are here and that is very wonderful.

Gertrude Stein was a household name. *In my generation I was the only one. The others, they are the incomprehensibles whom anybody can understand.*

Let's see, perhaps you will recognize this: *"Let me recite what history teaches. History teaches."* Hmmm, anyone??

How about this: *"Rose is a rose is a rose is a rose."*

Ah, a glimmer of recognition? *Now listen, I'm no fool. I know that in daily life we don't go around saying 'Rose is a rose is a rose'; but I think that in that line the rose was* red *for the first time in English poetry for a hundred years.*

How about this: *"They were regular in being gay, they learned little things that are things in being gay, they learned many little things that are things in being gay, they were gay every day, they were regular, they were gay, they were gay the same length of time every day, they were gay, they were quite regularly gay . . . "*

Ah ha. You may laugh but had you heard it before? Regardless I really do so appreciate that you came out here tonight to meet me, because even if you may have not read my books, you are curious.

And that, that is a very good start.
I am also curious to meet you in this way.
So let us begin.

> ALICE *sets up a lectern for* GERTRUDE.

> GERTRUDE *gestures to* ALICE.

My secretary.

> GERTRUDE *stands at the lectern.*

What is a genius. If you are one how do you know you are one. It is not a conviction lots of people are convinced they are one sometime in the course of their living but they are not one and what is the difference between being not one and being one. There is of course a difference but what is it.

I talk a lot I like to talk and I talk even more than that I may say I talk most of the time and I listen a fair amount too and as I have said the essence of being a genius is to be able to talk and listen to listen while talking and talk while listening but and this is very important very important indeed talking has nothing to do with creation.

The act of creation is about listening and looking, really looking, really seeing and capturing what you are seeing inside the continuous present.

Genius is about the way of seeing and seeing in a new way that is genius. There is nothing you can do about it, genius is yours or it isn't, you have it or you don't, you see or you don't see but of course the beauty of meeting a genius if you are not one is that a genius can of course change the way you see things.

If you had read my words I'm sure you would agree.

Is there repetition or is there insistence. I am inclined to believe there is no such thing as repetition.
I am inclined to believe there is no such thing as repetition.

It is funny this thing of being a genius, there is no reason for it, there is no reason that it should be you and should not have been him, no reason at all that it should have been you, no no reason at all. The only thing about it was that it was I who was the genius, there was no reason for it but I was.

> *Pause.*

It takes a lot of time to be genius. You have to sit around so much doing nothing. Really doing nothing.

> *A long silence while GERTRUDE does nothing. ALICE looks at the audience while smoking a cigarette.*

ALICE
Gertie. Ahem. Gertie—

GERTRUDE
I'm still doing nothing.

GERTRUDE returns to "doing nothing."

Another long pause. Finally, to the audience:

ALICE
Do you cook?

Long pause.

No leg of venison can compare with a leg of mutton prepared a week in advance. You must cover it with a wine, herb and virgin olive oil marinade. You see? *But the main point of the preparation is to arm yourself with a surgical syringe of a size to hold half a pint* you see—*filled with cognac and fresh orange juice. You must inject the mutton in three different spots three times a day for the week.*

Do you embroider? What about needlepoint? How extraordinary. What do you do with your hands, then? I made sure to keep my hands busy every moment in order to provide an environment in which a genius could flourish.

At our salons *I sat with so many* wives of geniuses. *I sat with wives who were not wives, of geniuses who were geniuses. I have sat with real wives of geniuses who were not real geniuses. I have sat with wives of geniuses, of near geniuses, of would be geniuses, in short I have sat very often and very long with many wives and wives of many geniuses.*

GERTRUDE
Ah, yes!

GERTRUDE has just made up this poem. She looks to the audience.

Some know very well that their way of living is a sad one.
Some know that their way of living is a dreary thing.
Some know very well that their way of being living is a tedious one.
Some know very well that they are living in a very dull way of living.
Some live a dull way of living very quickly and they are not then certain that they are living a dull way of living.
Some are coming to know very well that they are living in a very dull way of living. These go shopping.
They go shopping and it always was a thing they were rightly doing.
Now everything is changing. Certainly everything is changing.
They go shopping, they are being in a different way of living.
Everything is changing. In some quite completely changing, in some some changing in some not very much changing.
Everything is changing.

I wrote that in 1910.

ALICE
No baby it was 1911.

GERTRUDE
Oh of course boss, yes 1911, that's right pussy. *Everything is changing.* But genius, genius never changes.

GERTRUDE resumes her "doing nothing" pose.

ALICE
Gertie.

GERTRUDE
(whispers) Still doing nothing.

ALICE
(to audience) I will always remember the day I arrived in Paris in 1907 because it was the day I met Gertrude Stein. It was to be a holiday, away from the terrible earthquake in San Francisco you see but I never returned. On our very first night in Paris— my travelling companion Harriet Levy had been an intimate friend of Gertrude's sister-in-law Sarah Stein—Harriet said we should go see the Steins at their Saturday-night salon and we arrived and Gertrude was there. Gertrude Stein and her brother Leo were Americans living in Paris who were quite famous for their modern-art collection.

GERTRUDE
It was her lively eyes I noticed. I could tell she was really looking really seeing the paintings.

ALICE
Two Gauguins, the Toulouse-Lautrec, little paintings by Daumier and Delacroix, many Cezannes, enormous Picassos of the Harlequin period, two rows of Matisse, in short, everything. I was so much younger in experience. I wasn't so much younger in years—I was only two years and two months younger but it was the enormous life that she'd led, you could see—enormous power—she had such an extraordinary sense of life—I just drank it in.

With great energy and vigour, a younger version of herself, GERTRUDE is talking to a small circle of friends.

GERTRUDE

Gentlemen, gentlemen, gentlemen, gentlemen, gentlemen, gentlemen.

May I propose a toast tonight to new ways of seeing.

Henri, grab yourself a drink already will you? Can you tell me what it is about your painting that could be so irritating as to make one want to try to scratch the paint right off of it? I was there at the autumn salon and I tell you gentlemen and I am not exaggerating when I say this though from time to time I am known to do so but I am not now, that is what the people were doing: they were scratching.

But I loved this painting and so I put a bid on it immediately. Well luckily Matisse your paintings hold up to a good scratching, they are quite tenacious. Better to be infuriating and irritating than to simply continue to reproduce what is accepted to be beautiful. What is beautiful? Well Matisse, I say— To be misunderstood is better than to be standing under.

I like to collect geniuses and hang them on my wall.

You can look at these genius paintings for a hundred years and more and still see something new. Just as you can read my words for a hundred years and more and still see still hear something new.

So a toast tonight to Gertrude Stein: to my indelible legacy and irrefutable influence upon the foundation of modern literature. Cheers.

ALICE

She was a golden-brown presence burned by the Tuscan sun and with a golden glint in her warm brown hair. She was dressed in a warm brown corduroy suit.

GERTRUDE

Grey eyes hung with black lashes, her eyelids droop and the corners of her red mouth and lobes of her ears droop weighted down with long oriental earrings.

ALICE

It was unlike anyone else's voice, deep full velvety like a great contralto's, like two voices.

GERTRUDE

She's a gypsy her blues and browns and oyster whites.

Her heavy black Hebraic hair, her barbaric chains and jewels, her melancholy nose.

I marvel at her beauty I marvel at her perfection I marvel at her charm I marvel at her delicacy.

GERTRUDE extends her hand.

Ahem. Gertrude Stein.

ALICE
Alice B. Toklas.

They shake hands.

GERTRUDE

(to audience) I asked her if she would like to go for a walk the next day at the Palais-Royal Gardens.

ALICE

No baby it was the Luxembourg Gardens.

GERTRUDE

Yes the Luxembourg Gardens boss, that's right. But then of course you were late.

ALICE

Yes I was late but in the manner of the day I sent what everyone sent in Paris, a petit blue—I sent one ahead because I knew I would be late, just by half an hour.

GERTRUDE

It makes no difference to know ahead of time that someone is going to be late.

ALICE

Well most people—

GERTRUDE

I am not and never was most people.

ALICE

No my Gertie you never were most people. Remember how long I stood there in your doorway.

ALICE is at GERTRUDE's door. GERTRUDE opens the door, stands unsmiling and angry.

Hello Miss Stein, I'm terribly sorry . . . to be . . .

GERTRUDE is angry. ALICE watches her, confused, upset.

I am so—

Pause.

GERTRUDE
Now you understand.

ALICE tries to understand.

ALICE
I-I-I . . .

GERTRUDE
It is over. It is not too late to go for a walk.

ALICE
(to audience) It was the most important walk of my life.

*I must say only three times in my life have I met a genius, and a bell
within me rang, and I was not mistaken. In no way was I mistaken.*

GERTRUDE
(to audience) And that was the beginning of thirty-nine years
together.

ALICE
Thirty-nine years and seven months.

GERTRUDE
Yes birdy. Thirty-nine and seven. With never a day apart.

ALICE
Or even more than a few hours . . .

GERTRUDE
Yes lovey you are correct.

ALICE
And then . . . in Tuscany.

GERTRUDE
Will you marry me?

ALICE
Yes my king. Oh yes!

GERTRUDE
She cried tears of happiness for three days.

A Very Fine Valentine. Very fine is my valentine. Very fine and very mine. Very mine is my valentine very mine and very fine. Very fine is my valentine and mine, very fine very mine and mine is my valentine.

(seductively) Alice, What's for lunch?

   ALICE demures — not now.

Omelette in an overcoat.
Potatoes, smothered in butter.
Everything smothered in butter.
Red ripe raspberries.

Bavarian crème.

A fine fat poulet.

ALICE

(putting a stop to it) Mr. Potti.

GERTRUDE

If I am away from Alice I get low in my mind.

ALICE

(to GERTRUDE) Writing.

> *GERTRUDE begins to write.*

From the beginning *I was at home through Gertrude. Gertrude was the happiest person I have ever known.*

GERTRUDE

I have so much to make me happy. I know all that I am to happiness, it is to be happy and I am happy. I am so completely happy that I mention it.

ALICE

(to GERTRUDE) Writing.

(to audience) She must eat.

I cannot imagine any other life that would make me so entirely happy. I studied to be a concert pianist but I stopped because I knew I would never be good enough and the world doesn't need another pianist, but the world does need *(points to GERTRUDE)*. It was my devotion to Gertrude's genius that kept me going. *When she first gave me some pages of hers to read it was very exciting.*

When I taught myself to type I found my fingers were adapted only to Gertrude's words. It was like typing Bach.

GERTRUDE
I left my pages for her the morning after writing into the night. Alice's typing kept me writing.

ALICE
Gertrude's writing kept me typing. I typed for her and for everyone, for the future.

GERTRUDE
I wrote for myself and strangers, and the lined page.

ALICE offers GERTRUDE an apple.

ALICE
You must eat.

GERTRUDE
When you are lost inside the continuous present of creation you are more alive than when you are eating an apple. Because now you are still eating the apple but you are writing eating the apple and that tastes even better because now you are the apple and you both at once. Because you can be the sweetness and show the sweetness better than if you had said here try a bite of this apple, because by writing it you are the bite, the taste of the apple for everyone.

ALICE
A genius. A genius whom the public refused to recognize for far too long. For almost thirty years the cupboard was full of Gertrude's unpublished manuscripts, you see.

GERTRUDE

Publishers refused to publish me but I refused to stop writing books. They could not stop me. Nothing would stop me till I got there . . . even now it may appear that I am still trying to get there. Where? There. There? Where? *There is no there there.*

ALICE

Others did not recognize Gertrude's mind for far too long; they thought they did not understand her writing but they simply did not read it without worry; they would read her and they would worry they didn't understand her and so they were unable to enjoy her. I read Gertrude without worry from the very beginning and so I enjoyed her writing immensely and recognized that she had the greatest mind I had ever met and ever did meet, but it took a long time for others to do the same, though they did, in the end—they really did.

GERTRUDE

(reading) Dear Madame, "I really cannot publish these curious studies." Dear Madame, "I have only read a portion of it because I found it perfectly useless to read further as I did not understand all of it." "Dear Madame, I regret we are unable to publish *Three Lives, The Making of Americans, Tender Buttons* . . . Dear Madame, I regret, I regret . . . "

If you regret it dear sir then publish me and you shall have no more regrets.

ALICE takes a well-worn letter out of her pocket.

ALICE

And then there was this one. It was a scream.

(reading) "Dear Madam, I am only one, only one, only one. Only one being, one at the same time. Not two, not three, only one. Only one life to live, only sixty minutes in one hour. Only one pair of eyes. Only one brain. Only one being. Being only one, having only one pair of eyes, having only one time, having only one life, I cannot read your M.S. three or four times. Not even one time. Only one look, only one look is enough. Hardly one copy would sell here. Hardly one. Hardly one. Many thanks. I am returning the M.S. by registered post. Only one M.S. by one post. Sincerely yours, Arthur C. Fifield."

What an idiot. Even his imitation of you was pathetic.

GERTRUDE
There is a reason that I alone was the one to recognize and understand Picasso, and it is because I was expressing the same thing in literature.

ALICE
That's it, that's it exactly.

GERTRUDE
I was doing more important things than any of my contemporaries and waiting for publication got on my nerves. I wanted to smash the significance of the nineteenth-century order and structure, to shuck off old habits of seeing and describing, and to let a new art emerge.

I made twentieth century American literature.

ALICE
That's right Mount Fattie. You did and you did.

GERTRUDE
I made so much attractive literature with such attractive titles and . . . where oh where was the man to publish me in series?

ALICE
(to audience) As you will see in your program notes we published Gertrude's first book ourselves.

GERTRUDE
Three Lives.

ALICE
Perhaps this self-publishing will now seem to you that we were ahead of our time and so we were, in many ways I believe. But none of course none of us knew that then.

And now here we are, to set the record straight.

GERTRUDE
But of course eventually a real publisher eventually really published me: one thousand copies of *Tender Buttons*, by Gertrude Stein.

ALICE
Published by Claire Marie Press, 1914.

The reviews were less than favourable.

GERTRUDE
I have heard it said there is no such thing as bad publicity.

ALICE
(reading) "It is like the ravings of a lunatic."

"After reading excerpts of *Tender Buttons*, a person feels like going out and pulling the dime brick building over onto himself."

"The new Stein manner is founded on what the Germans call 'wort salad' a style particularly cultivated by crazy people . . . the way to make wort salad is to sit in a dark room, preferably between the silent and mystic hours of midnight and dawn and let the moving fingers write whatever comes."

GERTRUDE
The *New York Post* reviewer wondered if I had been eating hashish.

ALICE
(to audience) Unfounded rumours completely untrue. You may stop the hashish brownie rumours and jokes tonight. Enough is enough. Please check your program later for the full misunderstanding and explanation.

GERTRUDE
But back to my *Tender Buttons*.

I needed to completely face the difficulty of how to include what is seen with hearing and listening. Tender Buttons *was my first conscious struggle with the problem of correlating sight, sound and sense and eliminating rhythm. I was trying to live in looking and not mix it up with remembering, and to reduce to its minimum listening and talking, and to include colour and movement.*

Listen to this, an example:

(reading) Orange: A type oh oh new new not knealer knealer of old show beef-steak, neither, neither.

You see?

Rhubarb. Rhubarb is susan not susan not seat in bunch toys not wild and laughable not in little places not in neglect and vegetable not in fold coal age not please.

I was a little obsessed by words of equal value. Each part is as important as the whole. It is a realistic portrayal of everyday objects.

ALICE
Sausages.

GERTRUDE
Yes! Listen:

Sausages.

Sausages in between a glass.

There is read butter. A loaf of it is managed. Wake a question. Eat an instant, answer.

A reason for bed is this, that a decline, any decline is poison, poison is a toe a toe extractor, this means a solemn change. Hanging.

ALICE
Some were confused enough to think that "tender buttons" were *(muttering)* clitorises.

GERTRUDE
What?

ALICE
Clitorises.

GERTRUDE

Or marinated mushrooms . . .

ALICE

Or simply that Gertie liked buttons. But she was recognized as a literary cubist.

GERTRUDE

When I first began writing, I felt that writing should go on, I still do feel that it should go on but when I first began writing I was completely possessed by the necessity that writing should go on and on and if writing should go on what had colons and commas to do with it, what had periods to do with it what had small letters and capitals to do with it to do with writing going on which was at that time the most profound need I had in connection with writing.

ALICE

There are some punctuations that are interesting and there are some punctuations that are not.

GERTRUDE

Commas are servile and they have no life of their own, and their use is not a use, it is a way of replacing one's own interest . . . A comma by helping you along holding your coat for you and putting on your shoes keeps you from living your life as actively as you should lead it and to me for many years and I still do feel that way about it only now I do not pay as much attention to them, the use of them was positively degrading.

The fact of the matter is that those who are creating the modern composition authentically are naturally only considered of importance when they are dead.

(to audience) Why did you come here tonight?

ALICE

If you want to know my guess—

GERTRUDE

I always want to know your guess, even when I don't.

ALICE

Well then, it's the paintings.

GERTRUDE

Quite right, yes you are probably quite right—

(to audience) Alice is usually right.

ALICE

They could just read about the paintings.

GERTRUDE

Not a lot of readers in this crowd. I suspect they don't read much at all.

ALICE

(to audience) If you do read, not now of course, but later, you will read we lived as if in an art gallery—the walls covered from wainscoting to ceiling with pictures—only our pictures were more alive than most, the paintings breathed, the Gertrude Stein collection. The painting collection became well known and so Gertrude the collector became known.

But Gertrude didn't buy the paintings to become famous; she bought the paintings because she loved them and she saw what was contemporary in them, and even when the paintings became worth much more than we had ever paid for them, that never mattered to us: to us the paintings were our family, our children. We saw the future in them.

GERTRUDE

Our collection was what the twentieth century needed: a new art, a twentieth-century response, an art that acknowledged that time was different: movement, borders, communication, innovation: it was all different and art just like time cannot stand still. The nineteenth century was finished. These paintings were the present; they were the future.

ALICE

The paintings were just like baby's writing.

GERTRUDE

(to audience) Oh. You have been waiting for me to tell you about Picasso, haven't you?

"If I Told Him: A Completed Portrait Of Picasso"

If I told him would he like it
Would he like it if I told him
would he like it
would Napoleon
would Napoleon
would
would he like it

if Napoleon
if I told him
if I told him if Napoleon
would he like it if I told him
if I told him if Napoleon

would he like it if Napoleon
if Napoleon if I told him
if I told him if Napoleon
if Napoleon if I told him
if I told him would he like it
would he like it if I told him

"Gertrude Stein," everyone always says, "tell us about your famous friend Pablo Picasso."

I sat for ninety hours having my portrait painted by Picasso, every day for three months I sat and I could tell you more about that . . . but I am certain that is not the only reason you came here tonight, although certainly if Picasso was the one appearing then I suspect there would have been a great many more of you, but certainly I am hoping that having been a lion myself counts for something.

What is genius. Picasso and I used to talk about that a lot. Really inside you if you are a genius there is nothing inside you that makes you really different to yourself inside you than those are to themselves inside them who are not a genius. That is so.

And so what is it that makes you a genius. Well yes what is it.

Both Picasso and I *sought to express things seen not as one knows them but as they are when one sees them without remembering having looked at them.* We dismantled components of reality and reconstructed them. He with paint and I with words.

Certainly I will admit to you that it is more than a little irritating that later when he became very famous Picasso would not acknowledge my genius as I acknowledged his genius. He did not read my words as I read his paintings; he shrugged his shoulders and said it makes no sense, and frankly I have no more patience for men who shrug their shoulders.

ALICE
Hear, hear!

GERTRUDE
But there is so little time tonight and what I am really trying to understand is, *why was it that in my epoch, the only real literary thinking was done by a woman,* and yet why is my name not the one that comes to mind now. I suspect you have read Fitzgerald. Joyce. Williams. Pound. Hemingway . . .

ALICE
Hemingway was a pill.

GERTRUDE
I had a weakness for Hemingway. He was such a good pupil. And he did it all for my book *The Making of Americans. He copied the manuscript and corrected the proof. He learned a great deal doing that and he admired all that he learned.*

ALICE
There was more to the story than simple generosity. He entertained fantasies about you.

GERTRUDE
Ridiculous Alice. It was simply *so flattering to have a pupil who did it without understanding.* He said *writing used to be easy* before he met me.

ALICE
He was crude and insincere. He used four letter words and fabricated stories to make himself appear more virile.

GERTRUDE
That may be yet I still had a weakness for him.

ALICE
He told his friends he always wanted to—fuck—you.

GERTRUDE
What?

ALICE
He wanted to fuck you and you knew it. And that is a direct quote.

GERTRUDE
. . . I did not know.

ALICE
You knew it. You certainly didn't dissuade him.

GERTRUDE
All of this is absolutely your fiction borne of your tendency to a jealous nature.

ALICE
I do not have a jealous nature—

GERTRUDE
. . . May?

ALICE
As long as I am here and you are here you are not to say that name again.

GERTRUDE
You made me change an entire poem.

ALICE
They may lightly send it away to say
That they will not change it if they may
Just as May as in a way
May. May. May. MAY.

GERTRUDE
Alice I couldn't help it if her name happened to be an auxiliary verb. It is also a month. What was I supposed to do?

ALICE
You told me you never loved a woman the way you love me.

GERTRUDE
And it's true. Well anyway.

(to audience) Alice doesn't like Hemingway, so we don't like Hemingway.

ALICE
Well I got rid of him.

GERTRUDE, trying to be conciliatory.

GERTRUDE
Alice you have always had the most magnificent bottom.

ALICE
No no it is you who has the most fine bottom between us.

GERTRUDE

Your legs then your legs I insist your legs are the best legs. I know every curve of them and I would recognize your kneecaps in a crowd if kneecaps could be seen in a crowd.

ALICE

I would show you my kneecaps in a crowd if I could . . .

GERTRUDE

Alice what's for lunch?

ALICE

A flan of mushrooms a la crème.

GERTRUDE

A flan of mushrooms a la crème. A flan of mushrooms a la crème . . . a flan of mushrooms a la crème . . . a flan of mushrooms a la crème . . . hearts of artichokes?

ALICE

Butter. Everything smothered in butter.

GERTRUDE

Potatoes smothered in butter. Bread smothered in butter. *Omelet in an overcoat.*

ALICE

A fine fat poulet.

GERTRUDE

Pussy. Kitten . . .

ALICE
Mount Fattie, husband.

GERTRUDE
Mutton chops in dressing gown.

ALICE
Mr. Cuddlewuddle.

GERTRUDE
Wifie. My little Jewess.

ALICE
Red ripe raspberries, Bavarian cream. Triple-layer chocolate cake . . .

GERTRUDE
She was a magnificent cook.

ALICE pulls GERTRUDE down next to her.

"As a Wife has a Cow, A Love Story."

ALICE sighs — turned on.

In came in there, came in there come out of there. In came in come out of there. Come out there in came in there . . . as feeling as for it . . .

Not and now, now and not, not and now, by and by not and now, as not, as soon as not not and now, now as soon now, now as soon, and now as soon as soon as now. Just as soon as now. Just as soon just now just now just as and my wife has a cow as now, my wife having a cow as now, my wife having a cow as now and having a cow as now and having a cow and having a cow now, my wife has a cow and now.

ALICE

(overlapping GERTRUDE's text) Have it as having having it as happening, happening to have it as having, having to have it as happening. Happening and have it as happening and having it happen as happening and have to have it happen as happening, soon just as soon as now. Just as soon as—COW . . .

> *ALICE orgasms.*

GERTRUDE
My wife has a cow.

Did you like that there?

ALICE
Yes sir.

> *GERTRUDE turns to the audience.*

GERTRUDE
Did you recognize that one?

Perhaps some of you recognized that little bit of poem? It's from an excerpt "As a Wife has a Cow, A Love Story." Perhaps a great many more of you did not. But those some of you who did recognize, I suspect I may know who you are . . . Lesbians.

There I did it I said it. But. I never did use the term. Why must I? Read my work.

Have you read my short story "Miss Furr and Miss Skeene"?

"They were regular in being gay, they learned little things that are gay, gay." I use the word gay fifty times in that story.

ALICE
Published in *Vanity Fair* magazine in 1923.

GERTRUDE
That's right boss. That story of mine was apparently the first time the word "gay" was ever used in the press to describe homosexuality.

I will say I am . . . grateful to those of you who did carry my torch. And I appreciate a small audience, a dedicated yet small following. *Really to have the biggest publicity you have to have a small one, yes all right the biggest publicity comes from the realest poetry and the realest poetry has a small audience and not a big one, but it is really exciting and therefore it has the biggest publicity,* so thank you very much. *All right that is it.*

ALICE
I told Mr. Potty it was about time she wrote something that would be popular and make money. Many of the young men she mentored were doing far better than she was. Fitzgerald. Hemingway.

GERTRUDE
Remarks are not literature.

ALICE
(to audience) I didn't want to keep selling our "children," the paintings, to pay for private publishings.

I felt I was owed a little luxury. What with the shock of discovering "Q.E.D."—a manuscript about the aforementioned May, you can only imagine how hurt I was—devastated—simply gutted—never to have been told of this past lover—May—after thirty years together—I have said too much already. See the program notes about details which I cannot bear to repeat—I think it is fair to say I was owed a little luxury what with the shock of discovering—

GERTRUDE
You already said that Alice—

ALICE
I might say it fifty times if I like. I will say as I like. I will. And you will listen. And you will not say one word until I say you may. And I am the only one who will say the word may.

GERTRUDE
(cowed) Yes Alice, all right Alice.

ALICE is silent.

Alice.

ALICE
Yes.

GERTRUDE
May I— Can I speak Alice?

ALICE
You MAY.

GERTRUDE
Thank you Alice.

(to audience) So I did it. I wrote a bestseller—I did it for her. I just sat down and I wrote *The Autobiography of Alice B. Toklas* in six weeks. I just sat down and did it. Believe me it was not for pleasure that I did it. I felt the necessity to do it. I didn't particularly enjoy writing it. I did it for Alice. *If you love a woman, you give her money.*

ALICE
You do understand, don't you, that *The Autobiography of Alice B. Toklas* is not actually my autobiography. It was simply Gertrude's genius.

GERTRUDE
I wrote it *in my money style.*

ALICE
The general public bought *The Autobiography.* They bought it and bought it until they had to reprint and reprint again.

GERTRUDE
Yes everyone wanted to know about the salons, Matisse, Braque, Picasso, Hemingway. All of our friends. So I wrote about our friends . . .

ALICE
In the days before they were our famous friends.

GERTRUDE
Thank you Alice.

ALICE

" . . . one of the richest, wittiest and most irreverent books ever written."

GERTRUDE

"Lucid and shapely anecdotes, told in a purer prose . . . than even Gide or Hemingway."

ALICE

Ha!

GERTRUDE

While I was writing it I used to ask Alice B. Toklas if she thought it was going to be a best seller and she said no she did not think so because it is not sentimental enough.

ALICE

(speaks at the same time) No I do not think so because it is not sentimental enough.

GERTRUDE

And then later on when it was a bestseller she said well after all it was sentimental enough.

ALICE

(speaks at the same time) . . . well after all it was sentimental enough.

GERTRUDE

An overnight success—

ALICE

At the age of fifty-nine. And then *there was the spending of money.*

GERTRUDE

And there is no doubt about it there is no pleasure like it, the sudden splendid spending of money and we spent it.

ALICE

Everyone was reading her: storekeepers, bus drivers, school-teachers, housewives . . . everyone. However, Gertrude did offend some—Hemingway called it a "damned pitiful book." Check your program notes about the publication: "Testimony Against Gertrude Stein," signed by our so-called friends.

GERTRUDE

Some were offended by my descriptions of them. Well anyway. *Having written all about them they ceased to exist. That is very funny if you write all about anyone they do not exist any more, for you, and so why see them again. Anyway that is the way I am.*

But if you stop writing if you are a genius and you have stopped writing are you still one if you have stopped writing. I do wonder about that thing.

What happened to me is this. When the success began and it was a success I got lost completely lost. You know the nursery rhyme—I am I because my little dog knows me. Well you see I did not know myself, I lost my personality. It had always been completely included in myself my personality as any personality naturally is, and here all of a sudden, I was not just I because so many people did know me . . . So many people knowing me I was I no longer and for the first time since I had begun to write and what was also worse I began to think about how my writing would sound to others, how could I make them understand, I who had always lived within myself and my writing . . .

And I was not writing. Nothing inside me needed to be written. I began to worry about identity.

ALICE

I had never seen a time when my husband was not writing. This was the rhythm our daily life was built upon, lovey's pages, *the daily miracle*, the pages of longhand left on the floor that I would type out every morning. But for a time there were no pages.

Lovey there was never any doubt and there will never be any doubt. A genius is a genius is a genius.

Genius is not talent and genius is not success, genius is not pages: genius is genius, it is the way you SEE that is your genius so it does not matter whether you were not writing or you are not writing, it is neither here nor there: you were a genius, you are a genius, you will always be a genius. So in that case what is the question?

GERTRUDE
I marvel at my baby.

ALICE
Worrying is an occupation part of the time but it cannot be an occupation all of the time.

What about going to America . . .

(to audience) Her agent wanted her to go home to America for a lecture tour. *He said to her surely she wanted to get rich.*

GERTRUDE
Certainly I do want to get rich but I never want to do what there is to get rich . . . There are some things a girl cannot do.

And the food in America sounds very wet compared to French food.

ALICE
If we don't like any of it we will just go home. It has been thirty years.

GERTRUDE
Thirty years are not so much but after all they are thirty years.

Perhaps I could stand to write a few lectures.

When we arrived in New York—

ALICE
In 1936—

GERTRUDE
There was a sign lit up in Times Square that said "Gertrude Stein has arrived in America, Gertrude Stein has arrived in America, Gertrude Stein has arrived in America . . . "

ALICE
As if we did not know it ourselves, there was a sign to tell us we had arrived.

GERTRUDE stands at the lectern.

GERTRUDE
The creator of the new composition in the arts is an outlaw until the moment he becomes a classic.

A painting can be said to be ahead of its time and then eventually time catches up to it and suddenly everyone says it is a masterpiece as if the quality of masterpiece was always within it when at the time of its production it may have been called terrible and degenerate. *For a very long time everybody refuses and then almost without a pause almost everybody accepts. In the history of the refused in the arts and literature the rapidity of the change is always startling.*

So can a person be ahead of his time? I am here with you tonight and does that make me ahead of my time? Still ahead of my time? *No one is ahead of his time.*

What is ahead, what is behind and what is right now; what is it?

ALICE
But there is too much to tell about America. You can read about it later in the program.

GERTRUDE
It is very nice being a celebrity a real celebrity who can decide who they want to meet and say so and they come or do not come as you want them. I never imagined that would happen to me to be a celebrity like that but it did and when it did I liked it. We met Charlie Chaplin, Dashiell Hammett, Lillian Hellman; we were taken to the White House, we met Mrs. Roosevelt but the president was indisposed.

ALICE
Lovey . . .

GERTRUDE
We flew in an aeroplane to Chicago to see my opera, *Four Saints in Three Acts*. I loved flying! I loved it so much I told Alice B. Toklas that we should buy an aeroplane of our very own.

ALICE
(cutting her off) Lovey, they can read it later in the program.

GERTRUDE

Yes, if you came here tonight thinking we were going to tell you everything that happened then you were very much mistaken. What happened is only ever one part of what is important.

ALICE regards the audience.

ALICE

They are looking at us now with suspicion.

GERTRUDE

Yes perhaps a few of them, there have always been those who are suspicious of success.

ALICE

They are suspicious about more than your success Gertrude Stein. There were always those who were suspicious—the whispers, the looks. There are those who are suspicious in the way Gertrude Stein has been misconstrued.

GERTRUDE

Oh yes, there will always be those who will ask how did two women like us, two little Jews, survive two world wars. How do you think we survived? The way anyone survives a war.

ALICE

What were we supposed to do?

GERTRUDE

We were advised to go back to America during the Second World War.

ALICE

But anyone who left their homes in the last war lost them.

GERTRUDE

Paris in 1939 was not the place you might expect us to be but of course we didn't stay in Paris. We stayed out in the country in Belley where we usually stayed every summer but during the war well we just stayed there for several years instead of a summer.

ALICE

We never had any feeling of any minority. We weren't the minority. We represented America.

GERTRUDE

We were very friendly and of course I was very known and so we knew people, we knew many people, and so we knew people who knew many people and some of those many people were the right people to know.

I was the most famous Jew in the world.

ALICE

The Gestapo went into our apartment while we were in the country and pillaged and plundered all of the things that made our place elegant—our porcelain, our crystal, our linen.

GERTRUDE

But the paintings were saved—it was a miracle.

ALICE

They took our Louis XV silver candlesticks.

GERTRUDE
Alice—

ALICE
The little petit point footstool I made after the design by Picasso.
Beautiful.

GERTRUDE
(indicating audience) They don't care Alice—

ALICE
You didn't care—you never let me speak about what I lost, what
I cared about—

GERTRUDE
Did you not care about our paintings?

ALICE
. . . How can you even ask that?

GERTRUDE
Well then.

ALICE
You never once acknowledged—

GERTRUDE
The paintings survived. It was a miracle, a miracle.

(to audience) The Gestapo came with a truck to take them. They
had a list of pictures but they were driven out by the French
police because they had no papers to sequester the apartment.
It was a miracle.

ALICE

All those belongings meant something to me. And you knew it. And you would not let me speak of it, not even to mourn.

GERTRUDE

How could I mourn. How could I mourn about things . . . wifie. *We got off mighty easily.*

ALICE

You didn't know what had been taken. You said don't talk to me about it.

GERTRUDE

Alice you must stop.

ALICE

(to audience) Don't talk about it, please. Because of course she was right. But the rooms lacked the prettiness and elegance they had and sometimes I minded it secretly.

GERTRUDE

A Jew is a ghetto surrounded by Christians.

(to audience) Why did you come here tonight?

ALICE

Yes why did you come here tonight?

GERTRUDE

What did you expect to see and has it been that?

Ah and what happens when a thing is not what you expected?

What very often happens when you don't see what you expected to see is that the present moment is no longer present. It becomes the future or the past but no longer present, that is to say right now is no longer now.

And then we find ourselves asking is this a success or a failure. If it does not meet our expectations has it succeeded then, or failed.

And does that matter if you have enjoyed it.

Here you are; you have hardly read my words and yet you are here you have come out of your house you have come all this way and we have come all this way and here we are together tonight trying to know what it is to be who we are whether we are still here when we are no longer here.

What is left if you see what I mean.

Why did you come here tonight?

Perhaps you just like the idea of us: perhaps that is why you came, because you like the pictures, the anecdotes, the image of us: you were wondering how we remained outlaws in our own time and survived. You were looking for inspiration but you didn't want to work so hard as to read my books—I know some of it is difficult work and let me tell you I like to escape with a nice detective novel as much as the next person.

But I do believe that real art must express the struggle. If all you want to do is escape from struggle then why are you here? Art is not an escape. There is no escape.

You can try to escape, you can try to live a good life while all around you there is struggle unfolding and you can look away, turn off the war or turn it on, you can watch the past and the present and future all unfolding without punctuation, repeating and repeating you can tell yourself it is not your struggle you don't have to read my books but at least understand that you are standing on the shoulders of the thinking that was once and perhaps will always be difficult because the continuous present cannot be escaped and there is nothing easy about going down in history.

ALICE
I love you.

GERTRUDE
(to audience) Let me tell you, you can *write a book and while you write it feel ashamed for everyone must think you are a silly or a crazy one and yet you write it and you are ashamed, you know you will be laughed at or pitied by everyone and you have a queer feeling and you are not very certain and you go on writing.*

(to ALICE) Then someone says yes to it . . . and then never again can you have completely such a feeling of being afraid and ashamed.

Silence.

ALICE
After Gertrude died I typed; I typed till I could type no more for the day and then I would rise to type till end of day again. For twenty years I did that. *Everything Gertrude had ever written must be published and every publication with an article by or about Gertrude must be sent to the Yale library. It was deeply satisfying and a great comfort to me to know that* every word would be printed . . .

After Gertrude died everyone told me I should sell a painting . . . But they were our children, they were Gertrude. They needed to stay together.

GERTRUDE
She couldn't afford the heat you see, so she closed off all the rooms and ate her meals on a tray by the heater. I'm so sorry pussy.

ALICE
I sold a few drawings to pay to publish Gertrude but I couldn't bring myself to *figuratively burn a Picasso.*

Fifteen years after Gertrude passed I was eighty-four. That winter I went away.

That was the opportunity Roubina Stein and her children had been waiting for.

GERTRUDE
My sister-in-law.

ALICE
They went to court and had our art collection declared endangered—unguarded—by my absence. We had left the paintings many times on their own and they took very good care of themselves. If they survived two world wars they could survive a winter.

But they went in—the Steins, allowed by the law to break in like burglars, and took all of the paintings, impounded in the Chase Manhattan vault where I couldn't reach them. When I came home only the outlines were left on the walls. I remembered every one on those bare walls. The Gertrude Stein collection was gone. Our family was broken apart.

Perhaps you have seen some of them in art galleries around the world?

Jews don't believe in an afterlife but Catholics do. But after Gertrude died *I found I now believed that the past was not gone and nor was Gertrude. It left me in a dither when suddenly it came to me — where is Gertrude. She is there, waiting for us.*

So at the age of eighty I converted to Catholicism so I could be with Gertrude. In the afterlife.

Pause.

And oh, baby was so beautiful.

And now she is buried in the Père Lachaise Cemetery. I am too, alongside her. We share a gravestone. My name is on the reverse where I felt it belonged. You cannot see it from the path in the graveyard; you must walk behind to see it.

This is Gertrude Stein.

GERTRUDE
And this is Alice B. Toklas.

And so to end with, *thank you very much for everything and of course everyone is very welcome.*

When I first came to Paris it was spring.

When I came to Paris first spring was when I came, first I was in Paris and it was spring and then she came to Paris and spring came again and again she came and then again she came and came again and again and came again and spring became Paris and Paris became spring, Paris blooming in the hands of spring feeding Paris and Paris with an appetite blooming like the garden spring had planted in the heart of Paris, picking and eating Paris, spring feeding, blossoming becoming exploding with Paris in spring.

GERTRUDE *and* ALICE *depart.*

The end.

A NOTE ON THE CAHIER ("PROGRAM")

The blue cahier, included here with the play script, details some highlights of the lives and careers of Gertrude Stein and Alice B. Toklas. Throughout the play, the characters refer to it as "the program." Written by the Independent Aunties and designed by Kilby Smith-McGregor, the cahier is an essential part of the production of the play, and each audience member should be given a copy. For further information about acquiring rights to reproduce the cahier, please contact Playwrights Canada Press.

TIMELINE (of time)

ÉCOLE DE *IN CONTINUOUS*

DIRIGÉE PAR *PRESENT*

CAHIER

de *GERTRUDE STEIN*

APPARTENANT

à *Alice B. Toklas*

1927

1874
Birth of Gertrude Stein, Allegheny, Pennsylvania.

1877
Birth of Alice B. Toklas, San Francisco, California.

1880
Stein family moves to Oakland, California.

1893–1897
Gertrude attends Radcliffe College and studies philosophy, psychology and English composition.

Alice's formal education as a classical pianist comes to an end with her mother's failing health. *After mother's death Alice becomes the housekeeper for a household of men.*

1897
Gertrude fails her Latin exam and cannot graduate. She pursues her interest in psychology by entering Johns Hopkins School of Medicine. Sets up house with her brother Leo; together they host salons for relatives and friends of the Jewish intelligentsia.

1900
Gertrude's love affair with May Bookstaver, an unhappy love triangle involving another female student. *(GERTRUDE IS 23)*

1901
Gertrude fails four courses and cannot graduate.

1902
Leo Stein leaves for Paris.

1903
Love affair with May Bookstaver ends. Gertrude joins Leo in Paris, moves in with him at 27 rue de Fleurus, in the artists' quartier of Montparnasse. Begins writing "Q.E.D.," a veiled description of the affair. *Gertrude does not tell Alice about this manuscript until much later in life — AND ALICE REFUSES TO LET HER PUBLISH IT UNTIL AFTER SHE IS DEAD*

Gertrude begins writing first version of *The Making of Americans*. Completes "Q.E.D." *(unpublished until after her death)*

1903–1913
Leo and Gertrude share living quarters at 27 rue de Fleurus.

1904
(GERTRUDE'S LAST VISIT TO AMERICA FOR THIRTY YEARS)
Gertrude and Leo receive an $8,000 dividend from the family estate. In Paris they begin purchasing paintings.

PORTRAITS OF GERTRUDE STEIN

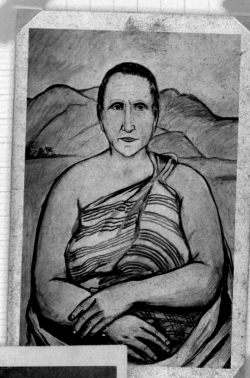

-Francis Picabia

--Pablo Picasso

HE SAYS
"IT DOES NOT
LOOK LIKE HER...
BUT IT WILL"

--taken by Man Ray
(1922)

1905
Gertrude begins *Three Lives*.
Introduction to Picasso.
THE SATURDAY NIGHT
SALON BEGINS.

1906
Gertrude sits for Picasso's portrait
of her. She completes *Three Lives*
and continues *The Making of
Americans*. Sarah and Michael
Stein, who have also begun to
collect art, travel to San Francisco
after the earthquake to look after
the family estate. They take some
of their paintings with them —
the first Matisse paintings ever
shown in America. Alice sees
the paintings, meets Sarah and
Michael, and plans to go to Paris.

- September 8, 1907
Alice and Gertrude MEET.

1908
Gertrude and Alice spend the
summer in Italy. —and
secretly marry
They return to Paris; Alice learns
to type and begins transcribing
The Making of Americans.

1909
Publication of *Three Lives*.
...published by the Grafton Press,
with May Bookstaver's help

1910
Alice moves in with Gertrude & Leo.

1911
Gertrude finishes *The Making
of Americans*.

1913
Leo moves out of 27 rue de
Fleurus. *FINALLY
The art collection is divided.

1914

Publication of *Tender Buttons*. Gertrude and Alice pay a summer visit to Alfred Whitehead in London. World War I breaks out and they cannot return to Paris until the fall.

1915 –1916

Gertrude and Alice flee zeppelin raids on Paris. *As a result of her isolation and concentration on the relationship with Alice, Gertrude Stein develops her specific language mixture of inner monologues and dialogues, her poetic "plays," and her "latant," if often disguised, eroticism...*

Gertrude and Alice rent a villa in Majorca. *WE MADE A VOW NEVER TO SPEAK TO A GERMAN.*

1916

Encouraged by the outcome of the Battle of Verdun, Gertrude and Alice return to Paris.

1917

Gertrude acquires a Ford automobile (Aunt Pauline*) and learns to drive; she and Alice volunteer to drive supplies to French hospitals for the American Fund for French Wounded.

NAMED FOR AUNT P. WHO ALWAYS BEHAVED ADMIRABLY IN EMERGENCIES

1918

After the ceasefire, Gertrude and Alice distribute clothes and blankets to the civilian population. Their active duty is later rewarded by the French government with the Médaille de la Reconnaissance française.

1919

Return to Paris.

1920

Salons are suspended for economic reasons, though the couple attend other salons such as the one hosted by Natalie Clifford Barney. Gertrude buys a new Ford, a sports car. *---NAMED GODIVA BECAUSE OF ITS NAKED INTERIOR.*

+1921 Gertrude secretly undergoes surgery to remove a lump in her breast.

1922

Introduction to Man Ray; photo sessions at his Montparnasse studio. Introduction to Hemingway. Publication of *Geography and Plays*.

("ROSE IS A ROSE IS A ROSE IS A ROSE")

1923

Gertrude and Alice become godmothers to Hemingway's son Jack.

1924

Gertrude writes *A Birthday Book* for Picasso's son Paulo. Hemingway arranges the serialized publication of a part of *The Making of Americans* in the *Transatlantic Review*. Introduction to Edith Sitwell.

1925

Publication of *The Making of Americans*. Introduction to Zelda and F. Scott Fitzgerald.

1926

First estrangement from Hemingway. Publication of *A Book Concluding With As a Wife Has a Cow: A Love Story*.

Edith Sitwell invites Gertrude to the Oxford and Cambridge literary societies; Stein uses the occasion to explain her writing for the first time, through the lecture "Composition as Explanation."

1927

Paintings by Picasso have become unaffordable to Gertrude; she is now interested in young painters. Gertrude writes *Four Saints in Three Acts*, an opera libretto for Virgil Thomson. In the fall, Thomson presents the first act of the opera to Gertrude and her friends.

1928

Purchase of new *(UNNAMED)* Ford sports car *AND A POODLE NAMED BASKET.* Gertrude writes *How to Write*, reflections on language, grammar, sentences and paragraphs.

• 1929

Gertrude and Alice rent "the house of their dreams" in Bilignin as their summer residence.

1930

First and only meeting with James Joyce arranged by Sylvia Beach. Gertrude Stein promises Georges Hugnet the English translation of his long poem "Enfances" *(BUT, INSTEAD, WRITES HER OWN VERSION OF HIS TEXT.)*

When this causes a breach in their friendship, she titles her version "Before the Flowers of Friendship Faded Friendship Faded."

Gertrude sells Picasso's *Woman with a Fan* in order to finance a publishing company, Plain Edition, that Alice directs in order to further Stein's work.

DOGS: Basket ii (top)
Basket & Pépé (bottom)

(NOTE: WE ALWAYS
HAD A DOG)

1931

The critic Edmund Wilson places Stein on the same level with Joyce, Proust, Yeats and T.S. Eliot. *(G.S. is 54)*

1932

Gertrude shows her agent the manuscript of her first novel, "Q.E.D." — *Alice had not known of its existence. It is about her affair with May Bookstaver.*

THE MANUSCRIPT IS PUT BACK IN THE CUPBOARD. it will not be published until I am dead.

Gertrude writes *The Autobiography of Alice B. Toklas.* *(COMPLETED IN SIX WEEKS)*

1933

The Autobiography of Alice B. Toklas is published and is a bestseller, Gertrude's first commercial success. She is temporarily estranged from Picasso because of Olga Picasso's dislike of the book, and her friendship with Hemingway ends. She buys a new Ford.

Gertrude experiences writer's block for the first time. *SEVERE IDENTITY CRISIS*

Plain Edition publishes *Matisse Picasso and Gertrude Stein with Two Shorter Stories.*

1934

Gertrude writes her first and only detective novel, *Blood on the Dining-Room Floor.*

World premiere of *Four Saints in Three Acts* in Hartford, Connecticut, followed by Broadway premiere.

1934–1935

Eight-month celebrity tour of America. Gertrude gives 74 lectures in 37 cities in 23 states.

Lectures in America include:

- "What Is English Literature"
- "Pictures"
- "Plays"
- "The Gradual Making of *The Making of Americans*"
- "Portraits and Repetition"
- "Poetry and Grammar"

Flew to Chicago to see Four Saints in Three Acts.

FIRST TIME FLYING IN AN AEROPLANE

1935

Gertrude and Alice return to Paris. Temporary estrangement from Picasso. First indications of WWII. — *Gertie refuses to believe there could be another war.*

(For safety reasons A ships copies of all G's work to Yale University)

EXCERPTS FROM
THE TESTIMONY AGAINST GERTRUDE STEIN

"Several of those mentioned in Gertrude Stein's memoir AUTOBIOGRAPHY OF ALICE B. TOKLAS find that the book often lacks accuracy... and that Gertrude Stein had no understanding of what really was happening around her."

(THEY DO THIS SORT OF GETTING WORKED UP OVER LITERATURE SO WELL IN PARIS. OF COURSE THEY HAVE MISSED THE POINT ENTIRELY.)

Absolute jealousy. —A.

FURTHER QUOTE FROM
THE TESTIMONY AGAINST GERTRUDE STEIN

"THE AUTOBIOGRAPHY OF ALICE B. TOKLAS in its hollow, tinsel bohemianism and egocentric deformations, may very well become one day the symbol of the decadence that hovers over contemporary literature. The testimony that follows invalidates the claim of the Toklas-Stein memorial that Miss Stein was in any way concerned with the shaping of the epoch she attempts to describe. PARIS, 1934.

SIGNED: Henri Matisse, Eugene & Maria Jolas, André Salmon, Georges Braque, Tristan Tzara...

"TESTIMONY AGAINST GERTRUDE STEIN" (attacks by Henri Matisse, Georges Braque, Tristan Tzara, André Salmon and Maria and Eugene Jolas) is published in *Transitions* magazine.

Alighting from a plane during their triumphant tour of the United States | c. 1934

1939

After France declares war, Gertrude and Alice close the apartment in Paris and decide to winter in the country. Gertrude receives a warning from the American consulate to leave France, but they stay. Stein writes her homage to Paris, *Paris France*.

1936

Gertrude Stein lectures again in Oxford and Cambridge. Introduction to Cecil Beaton, who takes photographs of Gertrude and Alice at his studio. Gertrude begins *Everybody's Autobiography*.

First Indications of the Coming War 1937 +

Premiere of *The Wedding Bouquet*, ballet based on Stein's "They Must. Be Wedded. To Their Wife," by Sir Frederick Ashton at Sadler's Wells Theatre. The lease at 27 rue de Fleurus expires. Publication of *Everybody's Autobiography*.

1938

Move to 5 rue Christine, in St. Germain. Gertrude writes for Picasso the play *Doctor Faustus Lights the Lights*, and a children's book. Death of Gertrude's brother Michael Stein.

1940

Publication of *Paris France*. Gertrude is advised to return to lecture in the United States or go to Hollywood to follow the prospect of a film version of *The Autobiography of Alice B. Toklas*.

On June 14 France is occupied. *Gertrude and Alice decide to wait out the war in Bilignin…* Stein writes *The Winner Loses: A Picture of Occupied France*.

1941–42

Gertrude sympathizes with Marshal Philippe Pétain's politics of the armistice. She makes an attempt at translating Pétain's *Paroles aux français*. A friend intervenes with the Vichy regime to secure the protection of Gertrude and Alice.

STEIN AND TOKLAS MANAGE TO SURVIVE THE MEAGRE YEARS THANKS TO THEIR VEGETABLE GARDEN, TO FISHING WITH THE HELP OF AN UMBRELLA, TO ALICE'S SKILL AT COOKING AND TO GERTRUDE'S BLACK-MARKET DEALS.

(Begining of G's third auto-biography: Wars I Have Seen)

1943

Gertrude and Alice ignore another urgent official warning to leave France.

The lease for the home in Bilignin is cancelled; they move to a new house in nearby Culoz that does not have a vegetable garden. Gertrude undertakes frequent mile-long walks in order to find something to eat.

They acquire a goat.

THE CEZANNE PORTRAIT
IS EATEN

1944

DEATH OF PEPE (THE CHIHUAHUA)
At the end of August, first American soldiers arrive in Culoz. American press reports Gertrude's "liberation."

She writes *In Savoy: A Play of the Resistance in France*. Gertrude, Alice and Picasso return to Paris and inspect the unharmed paintings at rue Christine. Short reconciliatory meeting with Hemingway.

1945

Publication of *Wars I Have Seen*, which becomes one of her most successful books.

A didn't type it up till after the war; knew the soldiers couldn't read G's writing anyway!

In June, Gertrude and Alice tour American military bases in occupied Germany.

They visit Hitler's country house in Berchtesgaden; the photograph is published in *Life*.

Gertrude writes a second opera libretto for Virgil Thomson, *The Mother of Us All*, about suffragette Susan B. Anthony.

Stein suffers attack of intestinal problems. — which she does not take seriously.

1946

Gertrude buys a new car, her last Ford. Another intestinal attack.

Stein is brought to the American Hospital of Paris in Neuilly-sur-Seine.

She makes her will on July 23 and leaves all her writings to Yale University and her Picasso portrait to New York's Metropolitan Museum of Art.

All else is left to Alice B. Toklas and, after Toklas's death, to her nephew Allan Stein; they are both named as co-executors.

This was to cause problems Gertie could not foresee.

Surgery takes place July 27; diagnosis of colon cancer is confirmed.

Gertrude dies under anaesthesia.

Alice continues to live alone at rue Christine.

1947
Death of Leo Stein.

1954
Alice publishes
The Alice B. Toklas Cookbook.

NOTE on the "Hashish Fudge":

This recipe was given to me by a friend named Brion Gysin. I was running late on my deadline for the cookbook and added the recipe without trying it or knowing what "canibus" was. There has been much nonsense subsequently made of this fudge, trying to shed light on Gertrude's poetry and our relationship and it absolutely incenses me---Gertude's genius was her genius and neither of us ever touched canibus or hashish or any of it.

Alice sells forty Picasso drawings without informing the co-executor of Gertrude's will. Allan Stein's widow, Roubina Stein, is very upset.

1957
Alice converts to Catholicism.

1960–61
To avoid the rigours of a Parisian winter, Alice stays for an extended period of time at a pension run by the Canadian Sisters of the Adoration of the Precious Blood in Rome. The landlord threatens eviction. Raid of Alice's apartment by the Stein heirs; they impound the remaining art collection. The Stein heirs agree to contribute to her income, but sums are often slow in coming. Old friends, including Virgil Thomson, contribute to her income.

1963
Alice publishes *What Is Remembered*.

+1964
Alice is evicted from her apartment and goes to live in the rue de la Convention.

1965
Alice suffers a fall and a broken hip and moves to a nursing home.

1967
Death of Alice B. Toklas.

GERTRUDE STEIN

1874 – 1946

ÉCRIVAIN AMÉRICAIN

Vécut ici avec son frère LÉO STEIN
puis avec ALICE B. TOKLAS
elle y reçut de nombreux
artistes et écrivains
de 1903 à 1938

This plaque still marks
27 rue de Fleurus

IT ALWAYS DID BOTHER ME THAT THE AMERICAN PUBLIC
WERE MORE INTERESTED IN ME THAN IN MY WORK.
AND AFTER ALL THERE IS NO SENSE IN IT
BECAUSE IF IT WERE NOT FOR MY WORK THEY WOULD
NOT BE INTERESTED IN ME SO WHY SHOULD THEY NOT
BE MORE INTERESTED IN MY WORK THAN IN ME.

THANK YOU

Brendan Healy for inviting the Aunties into residence at Buddies, programming the production and for the invaluable insight, belief and perspective on our work; honorary Aunties and collaborators Soraya Peerbaye and Suzanne Robertson; Mel Hague, Randi Helmers and Helen Yung for their essential creative support in the development of the play; Aunties patrons Blair Voyvodic and Chris Erikson (who opened their home in the countryside to us for a creative retreat), Luba Goy, Lee Pui Ming, Ingrid Randoja, Eve Goldberg and Ellen Long, Jane Orion Smith and Janet Ross; the Canada Council for the Arts, the Ontario Arts Council, the Toronto Arts Council and the Ontario Arts Council's Theatre Creators' Reserve (recommended by Theatre Smith-Gilmour, Theatre Passe Muraille and the Shaw Festival); and the amazing technical and administrative staff at Buddies in Bad Times Theatre. Thanks always to all of our families, especially Frida and Jim Ruxton, Liz Chatterton, Suzanne Robertson and Fox.

COMPANY HISTORY

Anna Chatterton, Evalyn Parry and Karin Randoja bring their individually distinct artistic practices together to create a unique and rich theatrical collaboration as the Independent Aunties. Dedicated to creating original theatrical work by and about women, the Aunties delve into women's societal roles, constraints and obsessions, both historically and contemporarily. They strive to create surprising, entertaining theatre with equal interplay between text and movement, heightened language, physical and imaginative style.

The Aunties have created six acclaimed, original plays together: *Gertrude and Alice* (Buddies in Bad Times, 2016), *Breakfast* (Buddies in Bad Times, 2010; Theatre Centre, 2008; nominated for three Dora Mavor Moore Awards), *Robbers' Daughters* (Cooking Fire Festival, 2007), *The Mysterious Shorts* and *Frances, Mathilda and Tea* (Theatre Passe Muraille, 2005), *Clean Irene & Dirty Maxine* (Buddies in Bad Times Theatre, 2006; SummerWorks Performance Festival, 2003, Winner of Best New Play; touring presentations in Whitehorse; Dawson City; Montreal; London, ON; Winnipeg; Halifax; Ottawa; Kingston; Rochester, NY; and Lansing, MI).

Anna Chatterton is a librettist, playwright and performer. A finalist for the 2017 Governor General's Literary Award for Drama for her play *Within the Glass* (Tarragon Theatre), Anna was named a top-ten Toronto Theatre Artist of 2016 by *NOW Magazine* and has been the recipient of the City of Hamilton Arts Award for Theatre and a Toronto Theatre Critics Award for Best Supporting Actress. Her solo play *Quiver* was produced by Nightwood Theatre and UNO Fest. Anna has been a playwright-in-residence at Nightwood Theatre, the National Theatre School of Canada, Tarragon Theatre and Tapestry Opera. As a librettist Anna's work includes the Dora Mavor Moore Award–winning *Rocking Horse Winner* (Tapestry Opera/ Scottish Opera), *Swoon* (Canadian Opera Company), *Crush* (Canadian Opera Company and the Banff Centre), *Voice Box* (Harbourfront Centre/World Stage), *Stitch* (the Theatre Centre, Dora Mavor Moore Award nomination for Outstanding New Opera) and *Sweat* (Centre for Contemporary Opera, NYC and Bicycle Opera/Urbanvessel, Toronto).

Evalyn Parry is the artistic director of Buddies in Bad Times Theatre in Toronto. Her award-winning, innovative and inter-disciplinary work is inspired by intersections of social justice, history and auto/biography. A theatre performer, writer, director and deviser, Evalyn is also a singer-songwriter; she has released five critically acclaimed CDs of original music, and a short film, *To Live in the Age of Melting: Northwest Passage*, in collaboration with Elysha Poirier. She is the winner of the KM Hunter Artist Award for Theatre, the Ken McDougall Award for Directing and the Colleen Peterson Songwriting Award. Her theatre-concert *SPIN*—about the feminist history of the bicycle—has had more than 250 performances around North America. Other recent theatre projects at Buddies in Bad Times Theatre include directing *The Youth/Elders Project*, the multi–Dora Mavor Moore Award–winning *Obaaberima* by Tawiah M'Carthy and writing / performing *Kiinalik: These Sharp Tools* with Laakkuluk Williamson Bathory. Visit www.evalynparry.com for more information.

Karin Randoja is a multi-award-winning theatre artist who has directed and dramaturged devised performance for almost thirty years. She graduated from the National Theatre School of Canada (acting) and went on a to be a founding member of Primus Theatre and the Independent Aunties. She has also been the director/dramaturge of such plays as *This Is The Point, Huff* by Cliff Cardinal (winner of multiple Dora Mavor Moore Awards, the Quebec Critics' Award, Buddies in Bad Times Vanguard Award for Risk and Innovation and the RBC Tarragon Emerging Playwright Prize), *Brotherhood: The Hip Hopera, My Nightmares Wear White* (winner of the SummerWorks Spotlight Award for Performance) and numerous other performances that have been nominated for the Prix Rideau, Dora Mavor Moore Awards, and the Capital Critics Circle Award. Her work has been seen in Australia, Denmark, India, Italy, France, England, Japan and Mozambique. As a teacher/director she has been a faculty member at Humber College for nineteen years, the Centre for Indigenous Theatre for four years and was a guest instructor at the National Theatre School of Canada for seven years.

First edition: March 2018
Printed and bound in Canada by Imprimerie Gauvin, Gatineau

Cover art and cahier design by Kilby Smith-McGregor
Inside cover art, *Insistence* and *Repetition* by Hazel Meyer
Anna Chatterton and Evalyn Parry's photos © Jeremy Mimnagh, and Karin
Randoja's photo © Kai Wa Yapp

Additional photo credits:

Page 55: Gertrude Stein and Alice B. Toklas, Aix-les-Bains, France, c. 1927,
from the Yale Collection of American Literature, Beinecke Rare Book and
Manuscript Library.

Page 57: *Portrait of Gertrude Stein* by Francis Picabia, 1933.

Gertrude Stein by Pablo Picasso, 1906 © Picasso Estate / SODRAC (2018).

Page 58: *Gertrude Stein and Alice B. Toklas in Their Paris Home* by Man Ray,
1922 © Man Ray Trust / SODRAC (2018).

Page 61: Gertrude Stein with Basket II and Marie Laurencin's portrait of
Basket II, c. 1940–46, from the Yale Collection of American Literature,
Beinecke Rare Book and Manuscript Library.

Alice B. Toklas and Gertrude Stein with Pépé and Basket I, c. 1932, from
the Yale Collection of American Literature, Beinecke Rare Book and
Manuscript Library.

Page 64: Gertrude Stein and Alice B. Toklas by Carl Van Vechten, 1934.

Page 67: Joint graves © Gordon Brent Brochu-Ingram.

**PLAYWRIGHTS
CANADA PRESS**

202-269 Richmond St. W.
Toronto, ON
M5V 1X1

416.703.0013
info@playwrightscanada.com
www.playwrightscanada.com